Sunbathing in Cemeteries

Jessi Kallison

Author's Note

When I started this book, I felt dead inside most days in the PTSD aftermath of a violent attack. And the sun kept rising, despite my incredulity that the world wasn't as dead as I was. I put one foot in front of the other. One day at a time. One task at a time. And it all felt like sunbathing in a cemetery—not quite right, but making the best of it. I also got really lucky and have people who love me on the good days and the bad days. That kind of support is invaluable. So, there are some saccharine verses to take the edge off of my second volume. It continues through my journey of healing, my new marriage, and the legal proceedings surrounding my attack. Thanks for sticking with me, and I hope I made you feel less alone.

--Jessi

To Ben,

my best friend, my lover, my double shot of dark rum.

Contents

Aspirin Thoughts

You are full of regret,

letting what-might've-been eat you alive.

But I'm insoluble.

I'm prepared to turn around and start all over

until I don't have aspirin thoughts coating my mind.

If you want to live in a world of sighs,

pining and never doing,

you can live there alone.

Ties That Bind

I'm shrinking my world down to these four walls.

I had tendrils trailing to the UK,

to Japan, to nearly every united state.

Misty connections that evaporate if you show a light too brightly upon them.

But in these walls…

I can't chop the tethers.

I can't burn them.

I can't dissolve them in my bitterness.

So, I'll pour myself into what I can't lose.

This small slice of the world.

These walls. This room. This bed.

Worth It

Did I have to feel the chasm spreading in my bed?

Did I need to struggle raising three oh-so-close-together nerdlings on my own?

Did I have to learn not to flinch

when a fist went through the wall inches from my face?

Did I need to watch retreating backs

as I hyperventilated through panic attacks?

Did I have to go on so many blah, how-do-I-leave first dates?

Was that really the shortest path to you?

If so,

it was worth it.

Volume Within Recommended Levels
(Finally!)

You put me back to sleep

and let me stay there,

tip-toeing, silent steps.

I woke, and the world was blessedly silent.

No neighbor obsessed over an extra centimeter of grass.

No fence mending.

No bird chirps unrelenting.

You stroke my hair

and let me be enough.

The safety bubble enveloping me sets the world's volume to low.

And I laze in your warmth like a cat by a window.

Odin

My reluctant, four-legged guardian watches over me,

my own foo dog at the steps of the temple.

He's certain I'm terrible at protecting myself.

So, resigned,

he's at my bedside,

then nosing me down the stairs,

shepherding me to the rest.

I can tell he thinks I don't know how to belong to a pack.

And I didn't ask for a guardian,

but I feel the weight of his judgment.

"Look, Odin, I only just had a pack choose me back."

He chuffs, sure that my brain is broken,

because he doesn't know about hearts.

But his presence is something I can bet on,

his waiting by the window is sure,

when I have gotten used to everyone leaving.

Walk the Wire

I used to wonder what fresh hell each day would bring.

But there are no more hells.

I burned hotter and brighter than the demons

and kicked my way to the exit.

You can, too.

But the way on is a high wire with no safety nets.

Which Team?

After I recovered bodies with my rescue unit,
my dreams were absurd.

People fell from cat5 cables after attempting body rappels
into giant pits.

I'd bag a body, but not know who to send its trouble ticket
to——

Which team handles this? Network isn't going to want a
body.

And you ask why IT themes tangle with the dead in my
dreams.

My mind couldn't distinguish the hells.

Service Desk

Hell is a phone that never stops ringing.

And its network is offline often.

The demons are disguised as finance workers with end-of-month deadlines.

If they can't reap souls because the lines are down,

they'll take yours.

…For answering the phone.

Insomnia

I lie awake,

wondering if I pull on any threads,

will we unravel?

How tightly are we woven?

If I shine a light in any dark spot,

will I find a knot?

Will I make a hole

if I try to untangle it?

Is that the color of our tapestry or a stain?

Are we too delicate to clean?

Will I bleach our details out?

Is there actually any flaw to obsess about?

I lie awake with Doubt between us.

He sinks his tendrils in,

dyes our story shades of blue.

I dye them back in a war of hues.

All while you sleep.

Zoom In

Nothing is the same

now that you're here.

Even my lint screen yields tiny clues.

Darker than before.

More sand. More dirt.

And dog hair. Sighs.

Layers of dog hair.

And it's cleaned more often,

you know, before it's a fire hazard.

If you change something so small as a lint screen,

I wonder what the rest of the world sees?

Hyperacusis

I think someone is hitting our counter.

And I ask you to check downstairs.

And I'm so sure I'm right.

I argue until you show me…

that the sound only happens when the dog breathes out.

YouTubers blaring that we should "smash that button"

make me want to smash my eardrums.

I can't think around it.

I flinch when you hammer a stud into place.

And I'm back against a door that's splintering around me,

buying my family more time.

So, you find me now before you hammer, drill, nail, saw,

decibel warnings far below the prescribed level litter our days.

You hand me noise cancelling headphones

like a life ring for the drowning.

And I hold on.

I ask you each time, "Will it ever get better?"

And you always say yes.

I don't care if it's truth or a lie

or only what you believe.

It's enough.

If Sherlock Made a Gratitude List

I scribbled items onto a gratitude list.

Like the experts suggest.

I needed a shift in perspective,

and my thoughts jumbled,

like a Sherlockian, who's-the-killer map.

Ideas connected with scarlet yarn pinned to a wall,

always looping back to you

in one giant web of thank you.

When the Future Went Dark

My future went black for a while,

and I put one foot in front of the other,

walking blind.

I didn't know what I was living for,

but my body didn't have the grace to die.

(Stubborn as I am.)

Semicolons and notes no one had to read

punctuated my nadirs.

Yet you picked me up each time I fell.

Today, I noticed the future is back.

The Future

I couldn't plan past an hour after I was broken.

I couldn't see myself doing anything but rocking back and forth.

No running. No hiking. No traveling. No painting. No writing.

I was trapped in the dark I-Can't.

Now I see a black wedding dress,

a kitchen big enough for both of us.

And we laugh, feeding our cave survey team.

We summit mountains I don't have a name for.

And we laugh after in our camper.

We scuba dive, seeing reefs other people won't.

And we laugh as we try to peel the wetsuits off our feet.

We raise kind, intelligent people.

And we laugh when they say beautiful nonsense and wreck our days.

We both think we are the luckiest.

False Beliefs

I believed The Devil over time.

I believed the terrible things he said about me.

And I began to wonder how anyone wanted me.

I believed no one else would.

And if I was so awful,

then maybe I deserved him.

He punched the wall.

I deserved that.

He broke my things.

I deserved that.

He broke me.

I deserved that.

I've served my penance in a hundred miserable ways.

I kept words trapped inside of me, un-writing.

I didn't allow my eyes to roam over the beautiful words

that other broken wordsmiths wrote.

I didn't let myself venture underground.

No sparkling speleothems to soak in.

I starved myself of beauty.

I deserved that.

And then the angel came along and wanted what's best for me.

In every way.

He loves my freckles, my scars, the delicate way I snore,

my hellbent-on-success, impossible goal lists,

my damn-the-torpedoes approach to life.

And I get to put on a sequined shirt, a leather skirt, a hot pink jacket.

To open the books I'd hoarded for when I was good enough.

To write each day like it's my last, and the ink is endless.

To linger underground.

To be happy.

I deserve that.

Almost Unbreakable

I've seen you hoist dressers that would break me.

And you spackle walls and replace rotten boards,

like you can erase neglect and abuse with sheer force of will.

You slip into my panic closet,

instilling peace with your hands.

You could find someone less shattered,

less held-together. Just more together.

Sometimes you try a dad voice on for size,

grousing about lights

and fans whirring on every device.

But I see you heading out the door

after you saw the dog cuddling his leash.

You're not fooling me.

I fill that deep fracture of yours. The one we don't talk about.

Now the air doesn't rush through our broken places,

without reaching our lungs.

And we smile without blue lips,

without aches to grin in spite of.

25

Harnessing Rainbows

I am a muddle,

an iridescent patch of oil in a parking lot.

Maybe green—no blue—or purple from this angle.

Kiss me or don't.

Our stories collide

and make a future on this axis.

But spin me about

and my future matches his.

Or his. Or hers.

My facets send rainbows scattering across the room.

Red from this angle.

Yellow from yours.

And all the same light.

But if you know how to harness rainbows,

I could be yours.

Spider Silk

Spider silk is five times as strong as the same weight of steel.

But no one thinks its lightweight mesh is that clingy,

until they try to break its hold on their skin.

The spider silk and I are both told we are strong,

but strong doesn't mean unbroken or wanted.

Under a Microscope

You size up my new partner like a fresh new slide,

focusing on the sample,

wondering what he has that you don't.

Hemocyanic blood? Cell walls? Extra lengthy telomeres?

But I was never looking for anything different.

You just left me looking.

If you have to know why he's here and you're not,

it's because he chose to stay.

Brain Drain

"Education ruined her."

That's what they said about me.

"We don't need nobody with book learnin'."

So, I decided to leave.

I let the pages teach me

what no Mississippian would.

That old white men can only rule the world if we keep electing them.

That there are no less-than-humans.

That Jesus doesn't kick mixed people out of church for not being born white enough.

That separate is never equal.

"Education ruined her."

That's what they said about me.

"Those liberal colleges indoctrinated her."

But maybe universities attract the open minds they seek.

"She thinks she knows more than us."

And what if I definitely do?

I noticed the bad statistics and flawed logic permeating the arguments.

Did you?

I spoke for justice, for equality, for change.

But my voice didn't carry over the roar of opinion.

My facts fell before men who called me strange.

Ignorance is as good as knowledge in their dominion.

I let education ruin me.

You should do the same.

Blueberry Boy

I cringe at the price tag on blueberries in the produce section.

But those giant navy orbs with their waxy, silvery bloom are beautiful.

Unwrinkled. Perfectly ripe.

I don't even like them,

and I put them in my basket

because I crave a blueberry grin.

You squeal with glee when I reveal what I bought,

clutching the package to your chest—

a temporary summer hoard.

And your dimpled, all-teeth grin is as sweet as berries.

Stretch Marks

You call your mother every night.

We all need someone to keep our vocal cords from growing rust.

A flea market from the dead litters her house,

trinkets to remember her abusers by,

what she couldn't let go of made manifest.

She spoke about Katrina like it happened yesterday,

not fifteen years ago.

Sheetrock still draped from the ceiling towards the table—

a hurricane souvenir.

The wall crinkled around the windows

where the house's dams broke.

It cried. She cries.

They cry into arroyos left in faces and dust.

The trauma map is on the wall

if you know how to read it.

But no one slathers sheetrock ointment into the joints.

Yet you call your mother every night.

The Club

There's no glitter here.

And the lighting doesn't flatter.

But all of the alcohol you can pour is included with a lifetime
membership.

We all get our own photo shoots.

We're models you see—

> of blossoming bruises and chokers stuck to our skin.

We skip the lines—

> at the ER.

We take off our clothes—

> to don backless gowns.

We do interviews—

> with men who forgot their microphones.

Our breaths come in ragged gasps.

We have nights we can't forget

and friends who won't remember us.

I won't welcome you to our club,

but I'll tell those waiting outside to go to hell

when they say you earned your membership.

1 in 8

1 in 8 girls who witness domestic violence grow up to experience it.

I saw the tsunami coming for my daughter when I read that.

And I was desperate.

Those are not her stars!

I threw the tea leaves back.

Braced against the shore, I wrapped myself around her.

I drew a circle,

summoning generations of women who endured

punches, burns, neglect, and misplaced blame.

Men made us invisible shields for their egos,

and now we hold the line.

We inscribed "Never Again" on her soul

and shared our grimoire.

Darling, here's what we bled to learn.

Here's when to run.

Publication Day

I was scared to click Publish on the most powerful lines I've written.

And that's how you know you've penned a gut punch with the truth.

You pause and wonder if you'll be invited back for Thanksgivings,

on outings with your friends.

But if you can't be honest and be loved anyway,

that isn't love.

So, wrapped in my convictions,

I pushed my little book through Amazon's birth canal.

Lasts

I didn't think I was done feeling tiny baby kicks.

But I haven't felt them in nine years.

I didn't cherish the last time she nudged me internally enough.

I didn't love the way she smelled

and how tiny she was.

Not enough.

How could I have let the moments of lasts pass me by,

convinced there were more?

I'm Happy for You

You rejoice over hummingbirds invading your windows.

I try out the phrase you send me when my life goes on without you.

"I'm happy for you."

God, why am I choking on it?

Why does each word need coughing up?

And why do the pieces of each syllable burn in my throat?

Why are we eating glass?

You pick curtains and hang them up without me.

I read a book in peace.

I'm.

Happy.

For.

You.

Crunch. Cough. Slice.

And we're so damned happy for each other as we choke up our bloody lies…

and go for another bite.

Closet Chair

The beanbag's overstuffed and too big for its spot;

it's a chair for you and a bed for me.

Beige microfiber, in full fluff just below the lowest hanger racks.

It cradles my whole body, hugging me when no one else will.

It's one of the nicest things anyone's done for me.

You didn't try to drag me into the light, puffy-eyed and sniffling,

where you could pretend this isn't happening.

You didn't impose a timeline on my recovery,

never treating my panic like it's fleeting.

You pulled up a chair and invited me to be comfortable

while in pain.

Like a spouse settling into a hospital chair to wait out the night,

you settled in like you'd stay.

In the beanbag for two in my closet.

Some People Are Worth Melting For

Little eyes are pouring salty waterfalls at us.

"Olaf can't talk to me anymore!" she wails.

I didn't know that she even cared about Olaf or his battery-powered routine phrases.

His prognosis is grim to her.

His vocal cords have cancer, and his time remaining is a few crossed off calendar days.

I propose a thorough surgery to restore function.

He didn't get this way from chainsmoking, and I can fix it.

She questions the consequences, the scarring, the methodology.

"There's no seam near the button! Don't you think this is a delicate procedure requiring laparoscopy?"

We hash out an entire exploratory surgical plan,

yet no one can turn off her lacrimal glands.

"Lilly? What else happened today?"

Her lip quivers. And I also perform heart surgery.

Free Falling

I was trapped in the edge of a yo-yo

The string only went up to sadness and down to despair.

I searched for a way off.

It moved in the rhythm of your fickleness.

Up—you miss me.

Down—you don't need me.

I rose to crash.

And I won't sleep with despair when the vacillations end.

I give up as I've tried to calculate the ways off the track.

And I quietly rub the string against the shards of my heart.

I fall.

And it feels like hope.

Box of Paradoxes

As a girl, I watched the deacons of my church kick a teenager out for not being white enough.

And I thought about the prostitute whose feet Jesus washed.

Was she white and pretty?

Or maybe a little too old to keep turning tricks?

Was she baring too much skin?

Do you think the congregation knew she wasn't Julia Roberts in *Pretty Woman*?

Teenage boys who wore confederate flag belt buckles

got away with Skoal cans in their pockets and dipping in class

as a black principal kept a fragile peace.

I read too much and still don't know how to keep my mouth shut.

Those boys threatened to burn a cross in my yard.

And I enjoyed the irony of the perfect icon for the South— desecrating religion in flaming hatred.

There was a black homecoming court and a white one. Separate. Equal?

Somehow black girls didn't win beauty pageants.

We all drowned in the Barbie aisle standards. Don't be pale.
Don't be black. Be California tan.

I held my breath as black people walked into the big, monied
Baptist churches.

They're new and don't know.

We only have white Jesus here.

Black Jesus is down the road and his people like music better;

they don't torture it out of the piano.

Mississippi has everyone trapped in a box,

held in the hands of an average white man.

The borders don't look like cardboard,

but I'm sealed inside with everyone who thinks.

Its sticky tape residue clings to my skin like the red clay when
I run barefoot.

Magnolia perfume permeates the layers,

cloying like the dead.

And some of us write on the walls.

Some of us sing our heartbreak.

Some of us paint the chaos within.

Art is born in contradiction.

To the Worthy Man

I will be brave,

a protector you didn't know you needed.

I will defend you when others don't understand you.

I will see who you are.

I will be transparent.

I won't hide my needs;

I won't conceal my brokenness or sorrow.

I will care

when your days are banal,

when you cry and don't know why,

when you get sick and need a keeper,

when you are soul-weary and too tired to take a step.

I will be your complement,

filling the voids,

working as your partner to complete a household,

supporting hopes and dreams to build our life.

I will trust you.

In angry moments,

I will give you the benefit of the doubt.

I will believe you,

no matter how many others have lied.

And I will love you.

You already know that means I would die for you.

But on my darkest days, I'll live for you, too.

No matter what transpires, yours is the hand I'll seek.

Yours are the eyes I want locking onto mine.

I will love you.

Baggage Claim

"When are you going to marry my mom?"

my son asks over my head.

I am luggage at the lost and found,

waiting for someone to claim me.

I hear the non-answer.

Am I not good enough? Sane enough? Successful enough?

Enough, enough, enough.

The luggage tag is missing from my left hand.

And I spin on the carousel while the crowds disperse.

Burying Fairy Tales

The impoverished but plucky girl marries the prince.

Slice. Scoop. Thump.

The prince saves the girl who found herself cursed, captured, be-damseled.

Slice. Scoop. Thump.

Happily. Ever. After.

Slice. Scoop. Thump.

We're burying the fairy tales today.

The girl becomes a queen by working hard and taking the kingdom by storm.

The girl beguiles her own dragons and rides them away from the tower.

Conquering. Ever. After.

Un-Days

The days we used to celebrate become holes in the calendar.

Stay-away-from-the edge,

you-might-fall-in days.

Anniversaries that got crossed out—

absent champagne, flowers, and cards.

Birthdays that aren't

for people that aren't.

Days when the world stopped

and our lives fell

into a pit disguised as an ordinary day.

It's a dubious privilege of aging—

learning how to span the shaky debris over those holes.

I'll tell you my secret:

don't look down.

Worse

"You're getting worse."

I wrap my arms around myself,

as far as they'll go,

protecting my core like your words are hits.

But they don't keep coming.

I wait for the conditional get-better-now,

stop-panicking receding footsteps.

But there was no *or else*.

No *if-then*.

You pulled me closer as I apologized

for more things I can't help.

I might as well apologize for the rain, too.

And you stop my torrent

like a shut-off valve in the sky.

Glitter Girl

Did you know that glitter is tiny glass?

A sparkly fragment of look-at-me sand.

I think my girl is a glitter soul—

a wonder to behold,

fierce, confident.

But also—a pretty that will cut you.

Not Just Ink

I wove gossamer strands of my soul into ink.

I resurrected monsters, combined myths, and blessed hearts along the way.

Souls aren't finite.

They can be replenished.

Exhausted. Consumed. Purified. And reborn.

But I see the bits of me in this line.

That flaw.

That beautiful bravery.

And I am a kid on the first day of school—

shy, terrified, and hoping some of you love me, too.

Hollow

You're a to-do list I didn't finish.

And the sting of unpolished whiskey

chasing regret down my throat.

You're the empty seat next to me,

the unrelenting itch on my scalp,

and the impossible spot on my shoulder blades

where my wings should spring from.

You're a quiet "kiss me",

echoing in my skull,

and the onions stinging my eyes.

Expendable

PTSD slid past my doctor's lips like a death sentence.

If you can't keep working 40 hours…

If you don't work the right kind of job…

If no one will claim you…

You are expendable.

We don't call it banishment,

But we push the weakest to the fringes

and let treatable maladies—

strep throat, broken ankles, rocketing blood sugar—

finish them off.

That's what befalls the victims.

But we're civilized. Don't worry.

The attackers get three meals a day,

a roof over their heads,

and free medical care.

If I were a felon, would I matter?

Leaden Soul

My minutes are eaten by hours as I lie listless.

My lead soul is too much to carry.

And I've finally fallen.

People kept acting like anything was bearable if I distributed the weight correctly.

But it doesn't matter how you pack on a quarter ton.

Did you think if I just wore it on my front, my back, my head, that I would be fine?

And sometimes you can't put it down. Sometimes it's your soul.

Pause Is Two Sides of Stop

I thought I'd hit pause.

Not stop.

I thought I'd feel kicks from the inside again.

I knew I would smell the newborn aroma that reminds a woman she can lift a car.

Like coffee tells us we can stay awake a little longer.

I thought tiny fingers would grip mine.

But nine years have passed.

Men, time, and opportunities all offered polite rejections.

How did this happen?

From Your Viewing Platform

I'm a hot mess.

A unique, exquisite disaster.

And I rage at the world

because everyone wants to gape at the wonder of the Grand Prismatic Spring,

but no one wants it to exist in their living room.

Six Months

Is six months long enough?

You swept into my life.

I was reckless,

looking for someone to take me down.

And you did.

I let you close enough to kill me,

and you might yet.

I know the core of you—

and the crumbled parts, too.

You think you'll wake up and know when the moment is
right.

Like a lightning strike of inspiration that forces you to buy a
ring.

But moments don't have the grace to align.

Time houses those who fall and those who beat them.

I know what you don't:

We make the moments.

And if you always wait,

you lose more than time.

Petty Revenge

I could plant kudzu along your back fence.

You wouldn't know until it had taken hold.

I could blow dandelion seeds

like glitter straight into your yard.

Dirt could clog your culvert. Inexplicably.

And a pond could rise with a storm.

The occasional nail could find its way near your house.

And your tires go flat more times than you can count.

I read about termites and know you never hired anyone to protect your house.

Do you know we'd need a queen to take your house down?

(It seems fitting, right?)

Life Ring

"Or you could marry me."

I hate those words,

heavy with hope,

life rings tossed to me as I tread the water.

I tremble with exhaustion,

too stubborn to go under.

Wait for it. Wait for it. Wait for it.

But you turn away before I can articulate the simplest words,

saved by a pizza timer bell.

The tip of my tongue was pinned to the roof of my mouth,

trying to eke syllables out.

You return and unpropose.

"You're overthinking it."

How can I overthink, "Or you can marry me"?

You mean at some later date.

Eventually. Maybe.

And my legs falter.

Seeing my life ring pulled back is worse than if there never was a life ring.

Hope is heavy.

And it will drown you.

Trigger

"You must have done something to deserve it."

I want to put your thoughtless words on paper and watch as you eat them.

I hope you never meet the violently insane.

I fervently wish that you are never brave enough to think you can help them.

And I utter this blessing behind you,

like sage cleansing evil from the corners:

I hope you never go through months of therapy to realize *no one* deserves to choke on their own blood as they are strangled.

Cough. Expel blood drops. No air comes in. This is it.

No one.

If I Were a Dog

I have a friend who rescued a dog who'd been thrown from a
moving vehicle after it had already been beaten.

Unadoptable. Afraid forever.

And the dog still has a place to heal, to half-remember being
a normal dog.

I have another friend who took in a dog his brother blinded.

And he always regrets that the dog was injured,

damaged so before he got it.

He loves the dog as he is—milky eye and desperate affection.

I thought that if the world had people like that who could
love broken animals, then I might stand a chance.

But there are no people rescues.

Awareness

October is National Domestic Violence Awareness Month.

And I know you like to shine a light on the subject.

Last October, you gave me a special purple necklace for the occasion

and a new scar tattooed on my face.

Now I *always* have something to remember it by.

Oh, to only have one month of awareness…

Ignorance = Bliss

I saw a couple out for the evening,

each pushing a stroller.

They looked happy.

Like no one's told them the grim prognosis on marriage.

I'd give almost anything to not know that people say they love you and leave.

I wish them more than stubbornness;

I wish them magic.

Custody of Keys, Pt. 3

You've reclaimed your key before.

I've been lost in a haze of keys like daisy petals,

ripped off and flung to the ground.

He means it.

He doesn't mean it.

He means it.

You press a key into my palm.

I almost don't feel it in the numbness,

bracing to enter the too cold, too loud, too violent.

I glance at the metal.

It is and isn't.

An artful exchange—like spies—we haven't lost our touch.

I hide it.

No one knows I have such a relic.

I've always known it was the key to something holy.

But you've only begun to realize it's sanctuary.

And this time you meant it.

Time

"Time heals all things."
You cough this pearl of wisdom up at me.
But it's not a pearl; it's just a grain of sand.
And you're not as sage as an oyster.

How can a clock's ticking hands heal me?
If I'm lost in the eardrum-lancing tick-tick-tick,
will my memories fade?

What about wrinkles, gray hair, skin elasticity?
Wilting flowers? Sliced apples?
Ocean plastic? Cancer?

You feed some monsters hours and days,
and they grow.
Trauma isn't bank interest.

What No One Told Katniss

They didn't tell you your hearing would be better than everyone else's.

They didn't tell you that you'd shake from adrenaline.

They forgot to mention the way you'd explode over nothing.

Or that you'd have slept with Peeta, Gale, and half of 12,

if it released all of this adrenaline.

If it would let you sleep.

Smashing Pumpkins

I never liked pumpkins.

Pumpkin spice might as well be ear wax flavored jelly beans.

Carving them was a medium to bring art out of the untastable.

Until you smashed five pumpkin canvases into my door.

Bam. Bam. Bam.

An autumnal battering ram.

I can't "disarm you with a smile or cut you like you want me to"

without seeing stringy orange guts and wood splinter specters.

Without hearing children cry over pumpkins

when they are really crying over losing peace.

But I never liked pumpkins.

Inshallah

My mother's house was leveled by tornadoes in April.

No one worried

because everyone assumed she had insurance.

But I know the truth.

Six months later my sister's house was battered by the winds
of Hurricane Zeta.

But we're not the kind of family who sees and learns.

We all have to feel the oven coils ourselves,

just to see if it will burn.

And feel men's punches ourselves.

It's a singular stubbornness—

almost faith—

to think you have more strength than anyone before

until your bones break, too.

Tatters

Men whisper "I love you" and then use me up.

They dragged me like a favorite blanket, loved to thinness,

shredded the walls that held up our fort.

I still looked like a blanket, though well-broken in.

The kind everyone wants because it's soothing and soft.

More came along to snuggle in my depths.

And a few knew I might disintegrate in the careless places
they left me.

And they still walked away after I've been loved to pieces.

I'm Happy for You, Pt. 2

I'm happy for you.

I have to say the words because my face won't work right.

It's not mustering a smile.

And I can't eke out a squeal of delight or laugh in joy with you.

But I ought to.

Since my face has gone rogue, I fall back on the lie.

I hope you believe the words.

I'm happy for you.

Nightfall

As the sun falls down into the Earth,

my pulse hammers double time.

The world doesn't go to sleep;

it gets louder.

I breathe around adrenaline flooding my veins.

My body thinks we are trapped in a house,

watching the Big Bad Wolf break the door down every night.

Don't breathe. He might find you.

The blood bangs in my ears.

For…hours…every…night.

I am a ghost reliving a death that won't end.

People think I survived.

But I know I must have died.

I see myself being choked like I was out of my body when it happened.

A Christmas tree sits where I died.

And we are both undead.

What I Lost

I used to drift off to sleep in minutes and straddle canyons in caves.

I once liked being alone and deciding how to spend my day, with no input from anyone.

I thought people were good; now I know in my bones that they are not. So, I'm shocked when they are decent, like I'm witnessing a miracle.

I carry books with me, knowing my focus is shattered in my ground-zero house. I buy more that I can't read because I *won't* lose this.

Before My Attack (BMA), I drank for fun. Now, I mete out a nightly shot like medicine.

Family and friends thought me crazy and left. Almost everyone.

I once had career options, but many evaporated with my disease.

I loved running at night, BMA, but now I know I am hunted in the darkness.

I was so carefree in a grocery store. Now, I plan the trip like zombies are inside. Scan the parking lot. Scan the aisles.

I used to take my kids to the climbing gym, but they let devils in and make a hell out of walls with grips.

I once did yoga, relaxing with deep breaths. Now every inhale reminds me that I can't breathe out of one side of my nose. And my chest tenses. And I need a punching bag.

BMA, I looked in a mirror and liked who I was. Now the woman never smiles, her hair is silvery, and there's a scar across her face that won't fade.

What I Gained

I stare down giants and tell them they will treat me with respect.

I know I will defend myself now. I never did before. I've learned not all life is sacred.

I live with panic so much it doesn't panic me now. I can stare at death and make decisions to beat it.

The part of my brain that ached for everyone died. I can stare at your blood now like I stared at mine.

I can see where light should fall to fix cave photos now. Left brain details.

I appreciate backpacking, really a deeper love of no people, no sound, no sleeping at ground zero.

…A man who believed me when I said I couldn't live alone.

Hope Shelf

I can't turn pages in my house anymore.

Living here is standing at a chasm's edge all day.

Try to focus on the plot, the words.

Read the paragraph five times at lightning speed.

And start over again, remembering nothing.

But I buy more.

And I put them on my To-Be-Read shelf.

I hoard them against the day that I won't be here,

won't be like this.

This is a thread of me he can't have.

My hope shelf.

Broken Mothers

I waited for you to come back.

I'm stubborn.

I waited my whole life.

Men bent you, used you, made every day a fight.

It's hard to be a mom like that.

Yesterday, it happened.

You spoke to me like you could see me.

And you made Christmas plans like a mom.

You offered me all you could find.

And I cried because loading my car with sanitizing wipes, espresso candy, and gas money is something a mom would do.

It's nice to have you back.

Constriction

My mom said men never commit unless they are pressured.

And I imagined myself a boa constrictor, squeezing the life out of you until you gasped out a proposal.

Or putting you in an arm bar until you tapped out with a "marry me" that sounds like "mercy".

But why would I want a commitment I had to drag across vocal cords?

If a man doesn't need me like water in a desert, he is hardly worth the effort.

Death to Lists

I make to-do lists every day.

They used to spring me into action.

Grocery lists, meal plans, project lists, chores—a pile of neon sticky notes sending urgency to me in nanometers.

But my urgency alarm is broken now.

Nightfall is urgent. Every minute of darkness. Every crowd. Every black car.

When everything is urgent, nothing is.

I thought I could trigger the ghost of myself. Make her care.

But she likes to watch the cheerful colors smolder to shades of gray,

fixated on ash caught in the wind.

Affirmations

I've never believed in fake it 'til you make it.

So affirmations puzzle me.

Tell myself things I don't believe until I believe them?

If I didn't believe my abuser for years when he spewed lies,

why would I believe pretty fake ones I tell myself?

When I Knew Irrevocably

You left. And I could've gone somewhere else.

To someone else.

I could've buried my panic in pleasure, killed my pain with kisses.

But I didn't.

The other arms are not your arms.

The eyes can't look at me like yours,

like I am the whole world in a bed, trapped in a moment.

I can't find a print of your mind

or a replica of the way you solve problems I didn't know I had.

And though I have options, I really don't.

It's real.

Stuck

I'm stuck in love, and I didn't mean to be.

I am covered in its tar, and I can't escape its pit.

I tell myself I can.

And that you can find love just anywhere

so that I don't freak out about the fragile thing that trapped me

and crush it in a commitment stampede.

I tell myself I could go elsewhere like I can kill myself tomorrow.

But I don't.

Did you notice how I don't?

All

The broken parts that never ran right.

The pieces shattered by careless words.

The quirks that make you singular.

When I said I wanted it all,

you should know I mean the flaws and scars, too.

I think you imagined me consuming you,

not loving every molecule.

Closure

I waited for closure.

When I would feel done.

And I thought it would be words you said,

Finally something sharp enough to cut yourself out of my heart,

out of my memories.

But closure was never something you could do that was finally awful enough.

It was me slamming the door on you to save myself.

And the door holding this time because it's as strong as I can imagine it.

Why I Devoured All of the Books and Why I Stopped

When the world you inhabit is bleak and there seems no way out, escape into stories can be a reason to live.

When everyone in your life is petty and exhausting and you're starved for one human like you, stories can make you keep going.

I made up friends I fell asleep talking to, and I danced with fantasy, wishing my worlds were the real ones.

But when you emerge, when you've been strangled awake, you'll find you are in charge of your fate.

You kick the villains out of your stories until you don't need stories.

You build a world you don't need to escape from.

Wedding Days

Wedding doesn't mean much after you've seen marriage
unravel.

The first time, you're never going to do it again.

It's the only shot to get it right, and everything has to be
perfect.

The second time—it matters.

You want to believe.

But you have two wafflemakers because he might leave.

The third time might be a whim,

in a dress you already own with knots easily undone.

Creating a spectacle dies with faith.

Emergency Contact

I check single on medical forms.

I don't have an emergency contact.

I stare at that question like someone just asked me to
integrate the color blue if it's in a gerund mood.

Who cares most if you're hurt?

Who cares most if you die?

What if they all care equally little?

Can I be excused from this question?

Maps

Before Google maps permeated the world, when phones were bricks, I got lost often.

I didn't know what road I was on, what to look for, which was east or west.

I spent a lot of time wandering.

I didn't know back then that someone could map all of the roads and a disembodied voice—the soul of Google—would tell me where to go.

And I would still be lost.

The Shift

You shattered the world I lived in and me along with it.

And I hate you for all I've lost.

But you forced me to examine which things I would put back on my shelves, which people to let back into my life.

I've been scrutinizing every facet of my existence since you strangled the old life out of me.

Which clothes to wear. Which to keep. What furniture I love. Which books. Which foods. Which hobbies. Which friends.

My life was an inventory in journals.

And everything was wanting.

I wanted too little before—being a man's, being a quiet writer, being only a mother.

So thank you for the shift in perspective.

And fuck you as always.

Invincible

You say I'm strong and brave.

But I can't look at pictures of spiders.

I feel a pulse of fear going over edges with my 11mm lifeline.

I drink my panic away when night falls.

People confuse brave with nothing left to lose.

They both look invincible.

I don't blame you, lucky fool, for not knowing.

The Trappings

I like my gifts in wrapping, dragging out the moments someone cared enough to get me a present.

I like to hold the anticipation in my hands—Schrodinger's perfection.

I drag my coffee out over hours, savoring the taste of morning.

Possible and *potential* taste like strong lattes.

I love the stem cell moment of a full coffee cup. I could pack a bag and drive into the horizon.

I wait on a give-me-a-ring precipice with amorphous daydreams.

The moment is imminent.

And right now, it could be perfect.

I could love the ring.

You could say the words that drag assent from my lips.

There's so much beauty in a box of clay.

All you need is a mind for Could-Bes.

Dendritic Words

You don't have to tell me.

I already know.

You are overzealous about your passions, old enough to drive most away, and strong enough not to care.

People don't learn to commune with trees because other people were delicate.

No one takes up residence on the fringe without a story.

You don't gauge normal well. And I don't either.

My rubrics were all broken when my senses were ignited.

Were people always so loud? So callous? Are they angry?

I can't tell, so maybe I should go.

And you went, too.

And so did she. We three stand around a cookie tin, gingerly and amused, a sisterhood of survivors.

The Pit of the Swallows

Sometimes I get so happy with you that I close my eyes and search for my melancholy well.

Is the undying sadness still there?

Am I still hollow?

Yes. But more.

I am the pit of the swallows[1] and the jungle around it.

It's still here. But it's not all.

---

[1] The Pit of the Swallows is a real place. It is also known as Golindrinas.

Banff

What-might-have-beens are strongest when the possibilities disappear.

I could go to Canada, but now the border's covid-closed.

Pictures of Banff haunt me as I wonder why I didn't make Morraine Lake a priority.

So it was when I got engaged and men rued what they didn't want soon enough.

Insoluble

Be careful with the filtrate.

Rinse every bit from the beaker with deionized water.

Leave none of the insoluble behind.

I carry the almost-not-there residue like I carry the few who remain with me.

Carefully. Don't-breathe-hard-ly.

They can't be dissolved in tears or distance. So much is soluble in water.

My Brain Skipped a Beat

I searched for your title in my mental catalog.

I tried to explain to a classmate that you help me with trig.
Boyfriend is the word I lingered on out of habit.

But that's not true.

My *husband* helps me with trig.

I stumble over the word that doesn't leave my lips combined
with *my*.

And my soul is a cat who found a patch of sunlight.

Thermodynamics of Abuse

Did you know that energy is always conserved in a system
when you slammed your head into my face?

Did you know you transferred heat to me?

You did work to scar my face.

And my delta has never been the same.

I absorbed your worst, and now it flows through me.

You diminished yourself and filled me with potential.

A Letter to My Irises

I almost ripped you up last year.

I looked at your obnoxious leaves and heard thuds against my window.

Echoes of my attack.

Rhizomes sound like rocks when launched with sufficient force.

But I knew you'd been as abused as I had.

And your whole evolution is based upon never having quite enough.

You grow close to the top of the clay, exposing your nerves like I expose my sins,

both of us rooted in the red clay that stains us.

We're more alike than I thought.

And we both bloom, flaunting our fuck-you flowers to the world.

What If

What if I woke up tomorrow and started walking, leaving everything I knew behind?

What if I left the white carpet I hated for twelve years?

What if I owned no more high heels?

What if I possessed no ounces of makeup?

What if I stopped finding traces of abuse like a forensic scientist who can say "Abuser was here"?

What if I left the South and never came back?

Would the magnolias miss me?

Or the vowels I'd tried to accurately phonetically depict?

Will the great pits know I haven't braved their depths in a while?

What if I leave and don't fade? What if I fly?

My Museum

Gazing at spaghetti noodle speleothems, awed, I wondered how I would ever leave, ever stop.

But I've watched most of my loves die on pyres, their remains labeled in the macabre museum of my memory.

First marriage, 2006-2018 ACE

My wedding rings didn't burn. And I pluck them from the ash, setting them in Mawmaw's candy dish. Diamonds as pleasant as hard cinnamon candies with plastic wrappers fused to their surface.

Caving, 2011-2019 ACE

My rusted croll[2] didn't have the grace to melt when it so often refused to grasp the rope. Carabiners smudged with ash offer connections I no longer want, can no longer stand.

The Man I Loved More Than Myself, 2018-2019 ACE

He remains whole. You can't touch The Devil. The fingers that wrapped around my neck don't have the grace to die.

I let my fingers dip into the ash museum. I scorch everything I touch. I'm always on fire, but never burn.

---

[2] A croll is a piece of climbing gear that grips the rope on certain types of climbing systems.

Me Too

I believe you with your eyeliner cat's eye,

wine bottle latched to your hand, goblet neglected.

I trace your hothead Facebook rants,

launching missiles with no guidance systems into screens like confetti.

Insanity isn't a switch.

It's a stone hitting a windshield and cracks that creep at every stress until the driver can't see clearly through the shattering.

Apotheosis

Be Blessed.

That's how Christian women say, "Go fuck yourself."

They don't implore God to do the blessing.

You're beyond divine intervention, you see.

They hope you'll be blessed, but can't name or imagine a god who'd want to reward you.

Sloughing

Tell me, little snake, did it hurt to shed the skin you outgrew?

Did you leave it behind without a second thought?

(Like hair fallen from my head? Or fingernails that I clipped?)

I try to molt my way out of bad habits, out of people who gaslit me, out of friends who hold me back or like me best in moody failure.

Do you think about who you are becoming when you burst out of your old skin?

Can I do it with enough force that the past is dust raining around me, just cells I can no longer run back to?

Ring Strain

Ideal bond angles are fixed[3].

I can predict what I need when we share space.

But when you try to cram me into your idea of perfection,

I'm cyclopropane—

dying to burst from the strain of the ring.

---

[3] Cyclopropane is quite far from its ideal bond angle. 90° is enough strain that it would want to burst open during a reaction.

AluI

You broke me.

Bluntly, you cleaved me.[4]

And I put out all of the signals for ligase disguised as a person—

Profile pics, witty messages.

"Ignore my blunt ends. You look like healing!"

But all of the -ases are mixed together and become exes.

So many broke me in staggers and fragments.

And then I met him.

He didn't say he was ligase.

But he grabbed my pieces and forged new bonds.

Still, you can't expect abridged DNA to hold the same code, to create the same protein as it did before the break.

And I am not the same.

---

[4] AluI is a blunt-cleaving DNA enzyme. Ligases bind DNA pieces back together.

Winter Solstice 2021

Does the frost lick your veins like the post-op splints tickle

my nose?

Just a little too cold, a little too painful to sleep.

Does the darkness blend into your shot-in-the-dark soul?

I raise another glass, hoping your nights are long and that you
forget the wonder of the galaxy. (It's you who gobbles
nanometers.)

I hope you live in the winter solstice and can't see the fractals
in the frost.

I still stand—a tree in the pitch—awaiting morning's kiss. But I
didn't forget to watch the night undress the light of a
thousand stars.